PAPIER-MACHE FOR KIDS

SHEILA McGRAW

A FIREFLY BOOK

Edited by Kathleen Roulston
Big photos by Joy von Tiedemann
How-to photos, design and cartoons by Sheila McGraw

Canadian Cataloguing in Publication Data

McGraw, Sheila
Papier-mâché for kids

ISBN 0-920668-92-5 (bound) ISBN 0-920668-93-3 (pbk.)

1. Papier-mâché — Juvenile literature.   I. Title.
TT871.M34 1991   j745.54′2   C91-094990-5

A FIREFLY BOOK

published by

Firefly Books Ltd.
250 Sparks Avenue
Willowdale, Ontario, Canada
M2H 2S4

Published in the U.S. by:
Firefly Books (U.S.) Inc.
P.O. Box 1325
Ellicott Station,
Buffalo, NY
14205

Printed and bound in Canada

To Lionel

Acknowledgements

Thanks to everyone who worked with me on this book: Paula Ring, Joy von Tiedemann, Graham Anthony, Elizabeth and Jennifer McGraw and Jagan Hadida. Also thanks to the staff at Firefly Books and all of those who worked behind the scenes on editing and production.

Contents

Getting Started

What Is Papier-Mâché?

It's a craft that anyone can do. Paper and paste are all you really need to make large or small, crazy or serious sculpture.

The words papier-mâché are French and they mean "chewed paper." But forget about eating newspaper sandwiches for lunch, because this book will show you lots of *easy* ways to make animals, monsters, jewelry and other great stuff — no chewing required!

You can say papier-mâché the French way, "pap-ee-ay mashay," or the English way, "paper mashay."

What Does It Look Like?

It's hard and bumpy. Papier-mâché objects can *look* cuddly if they are made round and plump, but if you take them to bed you'll have crazy dreams from rolling onto a lumpy thing instead of a teddy bear.

Sometimes when you go shopping, you may see smooth, perfect-looking papier-mâché ornaments like fish or parrots, and you'll probably wonder why your projects don't turn out like that. It's because the ornaments in stores are made in factories by machines. Thousands of them are produced all exactly the same, whereas yours are made by hand and they are all different. That is what makes them special.

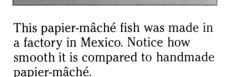

This papier-mâché fish was made in a factory in Mexico. Notice how smooth it is compared to handmade papier-mâché.

5

hy Use Papier-Mâché?

It's Cheap
Most of the materials that you need, like newspaper, flour, salt and water, are probably already around the house. Other items that you may need to buy, like masking tape and paints, are both easy to find and inexpensive.

It's Recycling
Using old newspaper to build a sculpture is a good way to recycle. You can also use other items that normally end up in the garbage, like paper towel tubes, plastic bags and bleach bottles.

It's fun to make new projects by looking at junk to see what it reminds you of — pie plates become a turtle, buttons are the eyes for a pig, lace decorates a mask, and so on — but

be careful not to use anything that is valuable or that belongs to someone else.

It's Easy
Almost anyone can make something from papier-mâché. It doesn't take much space or equipment to make all kinds of different things — big, small, crazy or serious.

You Can Make Big Stuff
All of the projects in this book are medium to large in size, because papier-mâché is one of the few crafts that lends itself best

to making big things. If you want to build a life-sized elephant, papier-mâché is the craft for you. Papier-mâché is often used to build props for the theater and huge floats for parades.

It's Fun
Get your parents and friends to help you, or have a papier-mâché party! Everyone loves this craft once they get started.

How Long Does It Take?

About three or four days for an average project, if you work an hour or two each day. Be patient. Time is needed for the papier-mâché to dry. Once the papier-mâché is dry, the project will need painting or decorating. The paint, glue or paste used for finishing will also need to dry. Plan ahead for school projects, because handing in a drippy, soggy project won't score big points with your teacher.

What Do You Need?

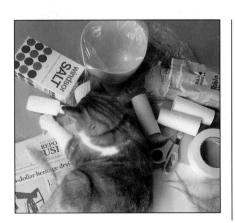

Not very much. Most projects require the same materials: newspaper, masking tape, flour, salt and water. Each project begins with a list of materials. Check first that you can get the things you need. When you have built your monster or spider or whatever, turn to the section at the end of the book called Finishing to see what is needed to complete your creation.

How Messy Is It?

Good news, Mom! It's messy, but not as messy as you might think — especially if you set up a good work area that doesn't need to be cleared off frequently. A card table works well. It's large enough and comfortable to sit at. Lots of materials can be stashed underneath it, out of the way, and it disappears when the project is finished.

When you have decided on a work area, cut open a garbage bag and lay it over the surface. Tape it in three or four places at the sides or corners. Don't work on newspaper, because your project will stick to it.

Although the flour and water paste will wash out of your clothes, it's still a good idea to wear old clothes when you work.

How Do You Do It?

Tearing Newspaper
Chase the cat off the newspaper and tear some newspaper strips. Most projects need strips about 1 inch (2½ cm) wide. Remember, paper has a grain. Tear it one way and it will tear straight and evenly; tear it the other way and it's a mess.

Cleanup
Placing a plastic bag in your paste bowl is a good mess saver. A used vegetable bag is good for this. Mix your paste inside it. When you are finished, throw the bag away and end up with a clean bowl.

Paste Recipe
• Place ½ cup (150 mL) of flour and a large spoonful of salt in a bowl. The salt will help to keep the paste from going moldy. Add 1 cup (250 mL) of warm water to the flour and salt.
• Mix it with your hands.
• It should be like thick, creamy soup. Add more flour to thicken it or more water to thin it.

Application
Spread paste on a section of your project. Lay a strip of newspaper on the pasty area. Spread paste on the strip. Lay a second strip overlapping the first one. Spread more paste on the second strip. Continue until the whole project is covered with 4 paper-and-paste layers.

To prevent print from the newspaper showing through your paint, add a layer of blank newsprint. Blank newsprint can be bought in pads or in cheap scrapbooks.

For some projects, it's easier to dip a newspaper strip in the paste first, removing the excess paste by pulling it through your fingers. Experiment to find which way you prefer.

Drying
Papier-mâché can take more than one day to dry. Try to allow air to circulate around your project to prevent mold from forming.

You can tell if the project is dry by touching it. If it feels cool, it needs more time.

How to Use This Book

Start with something easy if you haven't done papier-mâché before. The easiest project is the first one, Vases, which shows how to make vases from bottles and jars. They get more challenging as you go through the book, ending with the Monsters project, which is the most advanced.

Beside the instructions for each project is the Basics Box. It gives the paste recipe and other basic papier-mâché information. This means that you won't need to hunt for information through the book with pasty hands.

When your project is built and you are ready to paint or decorate it, look in the Finishing section for lots of great ideas.

If you want to make an original sculpture, look at similar projects for ideas and information.

Remember, the idea behind this book is having fun. Fun in the building, fun in the messy parts and fun in the painting. So flip through and find a project that appeals to you and get busy!

Vases

Flowers add a zap of color to any room! The vase that holds the flowers is just as important as the flowers in it, so create an original vase for a big bouquet or a single beautiful bud. Vases make great gifts for anyone — but especially for Mom on Mother's Day. Just add water and flowers!

How to Make a Vase

What You Need

- 1 glass jar or bottle, without the top
- Newspaper
- Masking tape 1 inch (2½ cm) wide
- Flour, salt and water
- Bowl for paste
- Blank newsprint (the kind you find in cheap scrapbooks)
- Carpenter's glue

Optional

- Plastic bag for paste bowl
- Toilet paper tube or other tube
- Scissors
- Corrugated cardboard

1 Make your jar more vase shaped by wrapping crumpled or folded newspaper around the threaded top where the lid goes on. Tape around it with masking tape.

2 Add more newspaper to any other areas of the jar to create the shape you want.

A toilet paper (or other) tube can be added to the top to make the vase taller. Tape it in position. The top can be cut at an angle, into points or waves, or left straight.

3 Corrugated cardboard can be cut with scissors into decorative shapes. Attach the cardboard shapes to the vase with masking tape.

4 Tear your newspaper strips about 1 inch (2½ cm) wide. Mix your paste. See the Basics Box for more information.

5 Spread paste over part of the vase. Lay a strip of newspaper on the pasty area and spread paste over the strip. Lay another paper strip overlapping the edge of the first and spread more paste over it. Continue until the whole vase has been covered with 3 paper-and-paste layers.

6 Add 1 layer of papier-mâché using blank newsprint. It will prevent print from showing through your paint.

When the papier-mâché is dry, waterproof the top of the vase around the opening by coating it with carpenter's glue.

7 Paint or decorate your vase however you wish. See the Finishing section for lots of great ideas.

8 Treat someone special to breakfast in bed with flowers.

Basics Box

Tearing Newspaper
• Newspaper has a grain. Tear it one way and it tears straight. Tear it the other way and it's a mess.

Cleanup
• For fast cleanup, place a plastic bag (a used vegetable or bread bag is good) in your paste bowl and mix your paste in it. When finished, throw the bag away.

Paste Recipe
• Place ½ cup (150 mL) of flour and a large spoonful of salt in a bowl. The salt will help to keep the paste from going moldy. Add 1 cup (250 mL) of warm water.
• Mix it with your hands.
• It should be like thick, creamy soup. Add more flour to thicken it or more water to thin it.

Application
• Be generous with your paste. Each strip of paper should be covered in paste so that they will all stick together.
• When working on small objects or tricky areas where parts join together, use narrow, short strips of newspaper.

Drying
• Papier-mâché can take more than one day to dry.
• Air circulation is important. Dry your project on a cooling rack, a heat vent or a radiator. Otherwise, rotate it once each day.
• Test your project by feeling it. If it is cool, it needs more time.

Bangles

Got a favorite outfit? Make a bunch of bangles to go with it! Papier-mâché is perfect for bangles, because it's lightweight and because you can paint and decorate it so many different ways. Cover your bangles with bold, bright designs or make them whimsical and romantic. Everyone will love your bangles, so make lots for gifts.

How to Make a Bangle

What You Need

- Lightweight cardboard (cereal box cardboard is good)
- Ruler and pencil
- Scissors
- Masking tape 1 ½ inches (4 cm) wide
- Paper towels
- Newspaper
- Flour, salt and water
- Blank newsprint (the kind you find in cheap scrapbooks)

Optional

- Plastic bag for paste bowl

1 Using a ruler and pencil, measure and mark 9 inches (23 cm) for a child's bangle or 10 inches (25 cm) for an adult's bangle onto the cardboard.

Measure and mark the width of the bangle. It can be any width you like between ½ inch (1 ½ cm) and 1 ½ inches (4 cm).

2 With scissors, cut along your drawn lines.

3 Bend the cardboard into a circle, overlapping the ends by ½ inch (1 ½ cm). Tape over the ends. Try the bangle on. Remember, when the papier-mâché is on, it will become slightly smaller.

4 To make the bangle thicker, take 1 sheet (or 2 stacked sheets for wide bangles) of paper towel and roll it tightly and smoothly, flattening the roll as you go. Stop when the roll is about the width of your bangle. Trim any excess.

5 Tape the rolled-up paper towel to the *outside* of the cardboard circle in 3 or 4 places to position it.

6 Continue taping until the bangle is covered in masking tape.

7 Tear your newspaper strips and mix your paste. See the Basics Box for more information. Narrow newspaper strips, about ½ inch (1½ cm) wide, will work best.

8 Dip a strip of newspaper into the paste. Remove some of the paste by pulling the strip through 2 fingers. Wrap the strip around the bangle. Repeat with another strip, overlapping the first one. Continue until the whole bangle is covered with 3 paper-and-paste layers.

Basics Box

Tearing Newspaper
• Newspaper has a grain. Tear it one way and it tears straight. Tear it the other way and it's a mess.

Cleanup
• For fast cleanup, place a plastic bag (a used vegetable or bread bag is good) in your paste bowl and mix your paste in it. When finished, throw the bag away.

Paste Recipe
• Place ½ cup (150 mL) of flour and a large spoonful of salt in a bowl. The salt will help to keep the paste from going moldy. Add 1 cup (250 mL) of warm water.
• Mix it with your hands.
• It should be like thick, creamy soup. Add more flour to thicken it or more water to thin it.

Application
• Be generous with your paste. Each strip of paper should be covered in paste so that they will all stick together.
• When working on small objects or tricky areas where parts join together, use narrow, short strips of newspaper.

Drying
• Papier-mâché can take more than one day to dry.
• Air circulation is important. Dry your project on a cooling rack, a heat vent or a radiator. Otherwise, rotate it once each day.
• Test your project by feeling it. If it is cool, it needs more time.

9 Add 1 layer of papier-mâché using blank newsprint. It will prevent print from showing through your paint.

10 Paint or decorate the bangle however you wish. See the Finishing section for lots of great ideas.

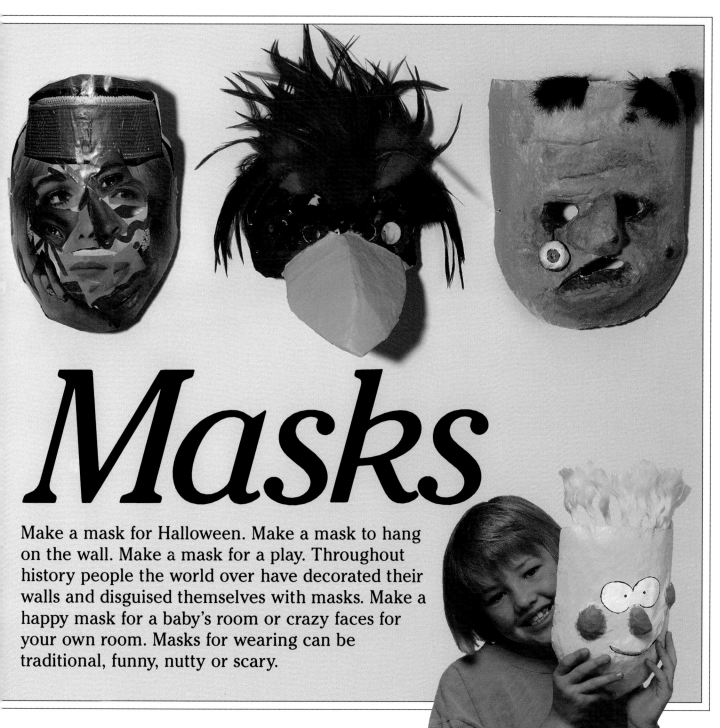

Masks

Make a mask for Halloween. Make a mask to hang on the wall. Make a mask for a play. Throughout history people the world over have decorated their walls and disguised themselves with masks. Make a happy mask for a baby's room or crazy faces for your own room. Masks for wearing can be traditional, funny, nutty or scary.

How to Make a Mask

What You Need

- 1 large, empty plastic bleach bottle (with a bulge on the front)
- Masking tape 1½ inches (4 cm) wide
- Pencil or pen
- Newspaper
- Flour, salt and water
- Bowl for paste
- Blank newsprint (the kind you find in cheap scrapbooks)
- Scissors or art knife
- Ballpoint pen or other sharp tool
- Narrow elastic
- Lightweight cardboard

Optional

- Plastic bag for paste bowl
- String for hanging

1 Remove any paper or other stickers from the bleach bottle. Make it as clean as possible.

2 Lay the bleach bottle down with the bulgy side up. Tape it to the table in this position. Try to keep it straight.

3 With a pencil or pen, draw the shape of the mask on the bottle. The rounded bulge will probably be the chin of the mask. Some masks can be the other way up.

4 Tear your newspaper strips about 1 inch (2½ cm) wide. Mix your paste. See the Basics Box for more information.

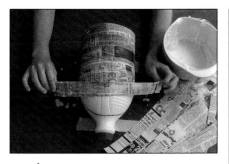

5 For the first layer of papier-mâché, dip a strip of paper into the paste. Pull it between 2 fingers to remove excess paste. Lay the strip across the top of the bottle. Repeat, laying the next strip overlapping the edge of the first. Continue until the whole mask area is covered.

For the second layer, lay the strips up and down the mask instead of across.

Apply 1 more layer with the strips running across the second layer.

6 Add 1 layer of papier-mâché using blank newsprint. It will prevent print from showing through your paint.

When your mask is completely dry, remove it from the bottle. It should come off easily. Do not try to pull it off while it is still damp.

7 With a pencil, mark the edge of the mask. Trim the excess papier-mâché with scissors or an art knife.

You may need an adult or friend to help you with steps 8 and 9.

Basics Box

Tearing Newspaper
• Newspaper has a grain. Tear it one way and it tears straight. Tear it the other way and it's a mess.

Cleanup
• For fast cleanup, place a plastic bag (a used vegetable or bread bag is good) in your paste bowl and mix your paste in it. When finished, throw the bag away.

Paste Recipe
• Place ½ cup (150 mL) of flour and a large spoonful of salt in a bowl. The salt will help to keep the paste from going moldy. Add 1 cup (250 mL) of warm water.
• Mix it with your hands.
• It should be like thick, creamy soup. Add more flour to thicken it or more water to thin it.

Application
• Be generous with your paste. Each strip of paper should be covered in paste so that they will all stick together.
• When working on small objects or tricky areas where parts join together, use narrow, short strips of newspaper.

Drying
• Papier-mâché can take more than one day to dry.
• Air circulation is important. Dry your project on a cooling rack, a heat vent or a radiator. Otherwise, rotate it once each day.
• Test your project by feeling it. If it is cool, it needs more time.

8 Hold the mask up to your face and, with a pencil or pen, mark where your eyes, nose and mouth are. Also mark the sides of the mask just above your ears.

If you are making a mask to hang on the wall, you won't need to cut eye, nose and mouth holes.

10 Using a ballpoint pen or other pointed tool, punch holes in the sides of the mask as marked. These should be at least ½ inch (1½ cm) from the edge. Papier-mâché around the holes to strengthen them or use binder-paper reinforcing circles.

12 To form a nose, cut a triangle from lightweight cardboard and fold it down the middle.

Tape it in place and papier-mâché over it with blank newsprint. Crazy noses can be purchased from joke stores and glued on.

9 Cut oval holes for your eyes and a triangular hole for your nose with sharp scissors or an art knife. You can also cut a mouth hole. NEVER DO ANY CUTTING WHILE YOU HOLD THE MASK UP TO YOUR FACE!

11 Cut a length of elastic. Thread the ends of the elastic through the holes. Knot the ends. Try on your mask again and adjust the elastic.

To hang your mask on a wall, tie string through the holes.

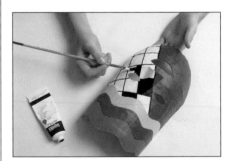

13 You can also decorate, add features or paint your mask. See the Finishing section for lots of great ideas.

Arachnamania

Crazy about spiders? For Halloween, or just for the fun of it, make some big pudgy spiders to scare the pants off unsuspecting visitors! Since a bunch of these creepy-crawlies are far more likely to be hair-raising than just one, it's a good idea to make several at once in different sizes and hang them in a group.

The legs of this spider are made from pipe cleaners. For big spiders, try to buy the larger size of pipe cleaners, available at craft stores.

How to Make a Spider

What You Need

- 1 plastic bag (a freezer-sized bag for a large spider or a sandwich bag for a smaller spider, not ziploc)
- Newspaper
- Masking tape 1 inch (2½ cm) wide
- Heavy black thread or string
- Flour, salt and water
- Bowl for paste
- Blank newsprint (the kind you find in cheap scrapbooks)
- Ballpoint pen
- Carpenter's glue
- 8 black pipe cleaners

Optional

- Plastic bag for paste bowl

1 To make the arachnid's body, fill the plastic bag with loosely crumpled newspaper. Push the paper into the bag and tie the open end shut.

2 Mash the bag until it is the shape of a flattened ball. Place strips of masking tape where needed to smooth any points and to help the flat ball keep its shape.

3 For the head, crumple a small ball of newspaper and tape around it.

4 Tape the head to one end of the plastic bag.

5 Tie the heavy black thread snugly around the body, leaving a long piece free for hanging. Hold the spider up by the thread to test its balance. Adjust it if necessary. Tape the thread to the body.

6 Tear your newspaper strips about 1 inch (2½ cm) wide or narrower. Mix your paste. See the Basics Box for more information.

7 Spread paste on your arachnid. Lay a strip of paper on the paste and spread more paste on it. Lay another strip overlapping the edge of the first strip and spread more paste. Keep going until the whole spider is covered with *only 2 paper-and-paste layers*. If you put more than 2 layers on the spider, it may become too heavy to hang up. Papier-mâché over the thread that is around the body, but keep the thread for hanging free.

8 Add 1 layer of papier-mâché using blank newsprint. It will prevent the print from showing through your paint.

Basics Box

Tearing Newspaper
• Newspaper has a grain. Tear it one way and it tears straight. Tear it the other way and it's a mess.

Cleanup
• For fast cleanup, place a plastic bag (a used vegetable or bread bag is good) in your paste bowl and mix your paste in it. When finished, throw the bag away.

Paste Recipe
• Place ½ cup (150 mL) of flour and a large spoonful of salt in a bowl. The salt will help to keep the paste from going moldy. Add 1 cup (250 mL) of warm water.
• Mix it with your hands.
• It should be like thick, creamy soup. Add more flour to thicken it or more water to thin it.

Application
• Be generous with your paste. Each strip of paper should be covered in paste so that they will all stick together.
• When working on small objects or tricky areas where parts join together, use narrow, short strips of newspaper.

Drying
• Papier-mâché can take more than one day to dry.
• Air circulation is important. Dry your project on a cooling rack, a heat vent or a radiator. Otherwise, rotate it once each day.
• Test your project by feeling it. If it is cool, it needs more time.

9 When the papier-mâché is dry, paint or decorate your spider body however you like. See the Finishing section for lots of great ideas.

11 Place a few drops of carpenter's glue in a hole and stick a pipe cleaner into it. Repeat for all of the legs.

10 When the paint is dry, use a ballpoint pen to punch 8 holes for legs.

12 Spiders like to live in warm, dark places, so find your spider a nice home.

Piggy Party

Why do people love pigs? Is it because pigs like to eat so much? Because they're pink? Or because they're funny looking? Pigs are perfect for papier-mâché. Their round shapes and big ears are easy to make. They make great gifts and fun ornaments, so make a bunch — a piglet extravaganza!

If you are making a flying pig, follow all of the directions plus the FLYING PIG ones.

How to Make a Pig

What You Need

- 1 plastic bread bag
- Newspaper
- Masking tape 1½ inches (4 cm) wide
- 3 toilet paper tubes
- Scissors
- Corrugated cardboard
- Flour, salt and water
- Bowl for paste
- Blank newsprint (the kind you find in cheap scrapbooks)
- Ballpoint pen or other sharp tool
- Carpenter's glue

For a Flying Pig

- Nylon fishing line or string
- Real or paper feathers

Optional

- String
- Plastic bag for paste bowl
- Ingredients for baker's clay (recipe, page 68)
- Ingredients for pulp (recipe, page 66)

1 To make the pig's body, tie the corners of the *closed end* of the plastic bag together in a knot. This will help make your pig body the right rounded shape.

2 Fill the bag loosely with crumpled newspaper. Push the paper down into the bag and tie the open end shut. If the end is too short to tie in a knot, twist it shut and wrap masking tape around it.

3 Mash the stuffed bag with your hands if necessary to get the best pig shape. Place strips of masking tape where needed to help form its shape or smooth out folds.

4 To create legs, flatten 2 toilet paper tubes and, using scissors, cut them in half across their width. Once they are cut, make the 4 halves round again.

5 Tape the legs in place on the pig. If they are not straight but angle out to the sides, loosen the tape on the outside edges. Stuff the tubes with crumpled paper and tape over the ends.

You can also tie string around, or attach tape to, the legs to help keep them straight. Stand your pig up to test its balance and adjust the legs if necessary.

FLYING PIG: The legs can be in any position you like. If you want the legs to angle backward (to make the pig look like it is travelling at great speed), cut the tops of the tubes on an angle before taping them in place.

6 Flatten and cut the remaining toilet paper tube however long you would like the pig's nose to be. Make the nose round again and tape it in place. Stuff it with crumpled paper and tape over the end.

FLYING PIG: Tie nylon fishing line or string around the body. Pick the little porker up by its string to test that it will fly straight. Tape the string to the body, but keep a length free for hanging. Watch out for string-chasing cats.

7 Cut out large piggy ears from corrugated cardboard. These should be a rounded triangle shape.

To give the ears more dimension, cut a V-shaped slash in the base of each ear. Squeeze it shut and tape it closed.

8 Tape the ears in place on your swine.

Basics Box

Tearing Newspaper
• Newspaper has a grain. Tear it one way and it tears straight. Tear it the other way and it's a mess.

Cleanup
• For fast cleanup, place a plastic bag (a used vegetable or bread bag is good) in your paste bowl and mix your paste in it. When finished, throw the bag away.

Paste Recipe
• Place ½ cup (150 mL) of flour and a large spoonful of salt in a bowl. The salt will help to keep the paste from going moldy. Add 1 cup (250 mL) of warm water.
• Mix it with your hands.
• It should be like thick, creamy soup. Add more flour to thicken it or more water to thin it.

Application
• Be generous with your paste. Each strip of paper should be covered in paste so that they will all stick together.
• When working on small objects or tricky areas where parts join together, use narrow, short strips of newspaper.

Drying
• Papier-mâché can take more than one day to dry.
• Air circulation is important. Dry your project on a cooling rack, a heat vent or a radiator. Otherwise, rotate it once each day.
• Test your project by feeling it. If it is cool, it needs more time.

9 Tear newspaper strips about 1 inch (2½ cm) wide and mix your paste. See the Basics Box for more information.

10 Spread paste on an area of the pig. Lay a strip of newspaper on the pasty area. Spread paste on the paper. Lay another strip overlapping the first one. Spread more paste on it. Continue until the whole pig is covered with 4 paper-and-paste layers.

When you papier-mâché around the ears, legs and nose, use narrower, shorter strips of paper. They will be easier to handle than large ones.

FLYING PIG: Apply only 3 layers of papier-mâché. Papier-mâché over the part of the string that goes around the body. Keep the string for hanging free.

FLYING PIG: Cut out wing-shaped pieces of corrugated cardboard with your scissors. Tape and papier-mâché them to the pig's back.

11 Add 1 layer of papier-mâché using blank newsprint. It will prevent print from showing through your paint.

12 When the pig is dry, paint or finish it as you wish. See the Finishing section for lots of great ideas.

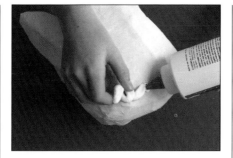

13 Make the pig's curly tail from baker's clay (recipe, page 68) or cut it from a piece of corrugated cardboard.

Poke a hole in the pig's bum with a ballpoint pen or other pointed tool. Put a few drops of carpenter's glue in the hole and stick the tail in.

Paint eyes on when the pig is finished or make them from either pulp (recipe, page 66) or baker's clay (recipe, page 68).

FLYING PIG: Attach real or paper feathers to the wings with carpenter's glue.

Yipers! Vipers!

Finally — here's a snake that's popular! He doesn't bite, hiss or slither and he doesn't swallow household pets or small children. He looks good too! You can make him chubby or skinny, curly or straight, and his mouth can be open or shut. Put a snake on Dad's desk or hang a group on a wall. Vipers on the bookcase, under the coffee table or peeking over the top of a kitchen cabinet are good for surprising unsuspecting guests! Don't forget to make one for your teacher!

How to Make a Snake

What You Need

- 1 wire clothes hanger
- Newspaper
- Masking tape 1½ inches (4 cm) wide
- Flour, salt and water
- Bowl for paste
- Blank newsprint (the kind you find in cheap scrapbooks)

Optional

- Plastic bag for paste bowl
- Wire cutters or pliers
- 2 old shoe boxes or tissue boxes
- Scissors
- Corrugated cardboard
- Ingredients for baker's clay (recipe, page 68)
- Ingredients for pulp (recipe, page 66)

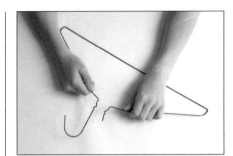

1 To begin creating the snake's body, untwist the hanger and stretch it out, except for the hook, which will become the snake's head.

If you want to make a shorter snake, use wire cutters or pliers to cut the hanger to the desired length.

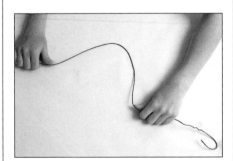

2 Bend the hanger to be as curly or wavy as you want the snake's body to be.

3 Crumple newspaper and tape it to the hanger with masking tape. Keep adding paper and taping it until the body is as fat as you would like, tapering the tail end. You may need a friend to help you hold and tape the paper.

4 To form the head with its mouth closed, crumple a ball of paper around the hook of the hanger. Tape around it.

For an open mouth, create two flat balls of paper. Tape around them, then tape them in place on the hook.

5 Tear your newspaper strips about 1 inch (2½ cm) wide.
Mix your paste. See the Basics Box for more information.

6 For the first layer of papier-mâché, dip a strip of paper into your paste. Pull the paper between 2 fingers to remove the excess paste. Wrap the paper strip around the snake. Do the same with a second strip, overlapping the first. Continue up and down the snake until the whole snake is covered with 3 paper-and-paste layers.

Read step 7 for a helpful hint before you papier-mâché.

7 It is easier to papier-mâché the snake if it is supported on two boxes about the size of shoe boxes or tissue boxes. This allows you to wrap the paper strips around the belly more easily, with less snake wrestling.

8 Add 1 layer of papier-mâché using blank newsprint. It will prevent print from showing through your paint.

Basics Box

Tearing Newspaper
• Newspaper has a grain. Tear it one way and it tears straight. Tear it the other way and it's a mess.

Cleanup
• For fast cleanup, place a plastic bag (a used vegetable or bread bag is good) in your paste bowl and mix your paste in it. When finished, throw the bag away.

Paste Recipe
• Place ½ cup (150 mL) of flour and a large spoonful of salt in a bowl. The salt will help to keep the paste from going moldy. Add 1 cup (250 mL) of warm water.
• Mix it with your hands.
• It should be like thick, creamy soup. Add more flour to thicken it or more water to thin it.

Application
• Be generous with your paste. Each strip of paper should be covered in paste so that they will all stick together.
• When working on small objects or tricky areas where parts join together, use narrow, short strips of newspaper.

Drying
• Papier-mâché can take more than one day to dry.
• Air circulation is important. Dry your project on a cooling rack, a heat vent or a radiator. Otherwise, rotate it once each day.
• Test your project by feeling it. If it is cool, it needs more time.

9 When the snake is completely dry, paint or decorate it however you wish. See the Finishing section for lots of great ideas.

11 Place the snake where it will receive lots of attention.

10 Using scissors, cut a forked, snaky tongue from corrugated cardboard, or make the tongue, teeth and eyes from baker's clay (recipe, page 68). Paint them, then glue them in place with carpenter's glue. The eyes can also be made from pulp (recipe, page 66) or painted on when the snake is finished.

Fat Cats

A chubby, touchable cat sitting on the windowsill or hearth makes a house a home. Because the shape of these cats is *so* cat-like, you can finish them in lots of different ways and they still look like cats. They can be painted realistically (to match your own cat) or with crazy designs.

How to Make a Cat

What You Need

- 1 plastic grocery bag
- Newspaper
- Masking tape 1½ inches (4 cm) wide
- 1 paper towel tube
- Scissors
- Flour, salt and water
- Bowl for paste
- Blank newsprint (the kind you find in cheap scrapbooks)

Optional

- Plastic bag for paste bowl

1 To form the body, stuff the plastic grocery bag loosely with crumpled newspaper.

2 Push the paper down into the bag and tie the handles together in a knot.

Mash the bag in your hands until it is a wide-bottomed pear shape. If it is too flabby, untie the handles and add more paper. Tie the handles again.

3 Place strips of masking tape around the bag in order to help form or keep the bag in the right shape. The tape can also smooth out points and folds.

4 To make the cat's head, crumple newspaper into a ball about the size of a grapefruit. Tape around it.

5 Tape the head ball securely to the top of the body.

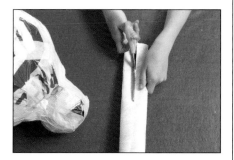

6 To make the legs, flatten a paper towel tube and, using scissors, cut it in half along its *length*. Make the 2 halves round again.

7 Place the 2 halves of the tube side by side on the front of the cat. They should be just below the cat's chest, with the cut edges against the body.

Tape across their tops. Cut the legs to the right length. Save the cut-off pieces to make ears.

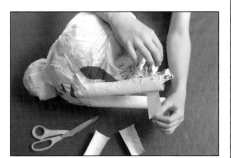

8 Fill the backs of the tubes with crumpled paper and tape around them.

9 Cut ears from the leftover pieces of paper towel tube. The tube will make them nicely curved. Tape them in place on the cat's head.

10 Create a tail by twisting and crumpling newspaper into a cylinder shape. Wrap tape around it.

Tape the tail under the cat's bum. Test kitty's balance.

Crumpled newspaper can also be added to smooth out areas, fill in areas or help the cat to sit straight.

Basics Box

Tearing Newspaper
• Newspaper has a grain. Tear it one way and it tears straight. Tear it the other way and it's a mess.

Cleanup
• For fast cleanup, place a plastic bag (a used vegetable or bread bag is good) in your paste bowl and mix your paste in it. When finished, throw the bag away.

Paste Recipe
• Place ½ cup (150 mL) of flour and a large spoonful of salt in a bowl. The salt will help to keep the paste from going moldy. Add 1 cup (250 mL) of warm water.
• Mix it with your hands.
• It should be like thick, creamy soup. Add more flour to thicken it or more water to thin it.

Application
• Be generous with your paste. Each strip of paper should be covered in paste so that they will all stick together.
• When working on small objects or tricky areas where parts join together, use narrow, short strips of newspaper.

Drying
• Papier-mâché can take more than one day to dry.
• Air circulation is important. Dry your project on a cooling rack, a heat vent or a radiator. Otherwise, rotate it once each day.
• Test your project by feeling it. If it is cool, it needs more time.

11 Tear your newspaper strips and mix your paste. See the Basics Box for more information.

12 Spread some paste on a portion of your cat. Lay a strip of newspaper onto the pasty area. Spread paste on the paper strip. Lay another strip overlapping the first one. Spread more paste. Continue until the whole cat is covered with 4 paper-and-paste layers.

13 Add 1 layer of papier-mâché using blank newsprint. It will prevent print from showing through your paint.

14 When the cat is dry, paint or finish it however you like. See the Finishing section for lots of great ideas.

Monsters

Make a monster to guard your room and keep the other ones — the ones that live in your closet and under the bed — from coming out to bother you at night. Make your monster friendly and funny looking, with googly eyes and crazy hair. Or make it as scary as you like, by adding warts and wrinkles or anything slimy or gruesome that you can think of.

How to Make a Monster

What You Need

- 1 plastic grocery bag
- Newspaper
- Masking tape 1½ inches (4 cm) wide
- 1 toilet paper tube
- Scissors
- Corrugated cardboard
- Flour, salt and water
- Bowl for paste
- Art knife or small, sharp kitchen knife
- Carpenter's glue
- Blank newsprint (the kind you find in cheap scrapbooks)

Optional

- Plastic bag for paste bowl
- Ingredients for pulp (recipe, page 66)

1 To form the monster's body, stuff the plastic grocery bag loosely with crumpled newspaper.

2 Push the paper down into the bag and tie the handles together in a knot.

3 Mash the bag in your hands until it is a flat-bottomed pear shape. If it is too flabby, untie the handles and add more paper. Tie the handles again. Place strips of masking tape around the bag to flatten points or to help keep the bag's shape.

4 Add crumpled paper to the top of the monster's body to make it even more pear shaped. Tape it in place.

5 To make legs, flatten a toilet paper tube and cut it in half across its width with scissors. Make the tubes round again.

6 With scissors, cut three-toed feet from corrugated cardboard. These can be big or small, rounded or pointed, however you'd like your monster's feet to be. Just be sure that there's a spot large enough to stick the legs on (see step 7).

7 Tape the tube halves to the cardboard feet. Stuff the tubes with crumpled newspaper.

8 Tape the tops of the legs to the monster's body in a sitting or standing position.

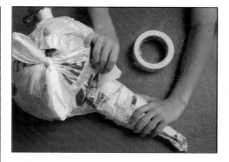

9 A tail will add stability to your monster, whether it sits or stands. Form a tail from crumpled newspaper. Tape around it. It should be tapered. Add paper and tape until it is a good monster-tail shape.

10 Tear your newspaper strips and mix your paste. See the Basics Box on the next page for more information.

Basics Box

Tearing Newspaper
• Newspaper has a grain. Tear it one way and it tears straight. Tear it the other way and it's a mess.

Cleanup
• For fast cleanup, place a plastic bag (a used vegetable or bread bag is good) in your paste bowl and mix your paste in it. When finished, throw the bag away.

Paste Recipe
• Place ½ cup (150 mL) of flour and a large spoonful of salt in a bowl. The salt will help to keep the paste from going moldy. Add 1 cup (250 mL) of warm water.
• Mix it with your hands.
• It should be like thick, creamy soup. Add more flour to thicken it or more water to thin it.

Application
• Be generous with your paste. Each strip of paper should be covered in paste so that they will all stick together.
• When working on small objects or tricky areas where parts join together, use narrow, short strips of newspaper.

Drying
• Papier-mâché can take more than one day to dry.
• Air circulation is important. Dry your project on a cooling rack, a heat vent or a radiator. Otherwise, rotate it once each day.
• Test your project by feeling it. If it is cool, it needs more time.

11 Spread paste over a section of your monster. Lay a newspaper strip on the pasty area. Spread more paste on the strip. Lay another strip overlapping the first one. Spread more paste. Continue until the whole monster is covered with 4 paper-and-paste layers.

12 When the papier-mâché is dry, you may wish to add points to the monster's back. With scissors, cut the points from corrugated cardboard and tape them in place. Papier-mâché over them.

13 Form short arms from crumpled, taped newspaper. Using an art knife or a small, sharp kitchen knife, cut 2 holes into the monster. Place some carpenter's glue in each hole and insert the arms. Papier-mâché the arms to the body.

14 Add 1 layer of papier-mâché using blank newsprint. It will prevent print from showing through your paint.

15 Eyes, horns, lips, ears, a big nose, warts or anything you think up can be made from pulp (recipe, page 66).

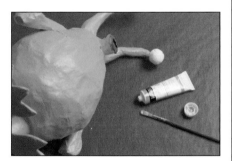

16 Paint or decorate your monster however you like. See the Finishing section for lots of great ideas.

Finishing

Now comes the real fun, changing your sculpture from boring to brilliant! While an imaginative paint job is a sure way to brighten any object, there are many other methods of finishing that are fast, fun and rewarding. So gather up the materials you'll need and get started. This is the quickest and most gratifying part of the whole thing!

Painting Papier-Mâché

The bumpy surface of papier-mâché won't let you do a perfect paint job with smooth edges and even shading, so start with a fun, simple, bold idea to avoid frustration. Then play and have fun with your paint!

What You Need

Acrylic paints are the best paints to use; however, tempera paints or poster paints can be used if you mix them with some podgy (available at craft stores) or some carpenter's glue to make them waterproof when they are dry.

   Don't buy expensive brushes, because the rough texture of the papier-mâché will break the bristles. Inexpensive ones are fine. You will probably need a variety of sizes.

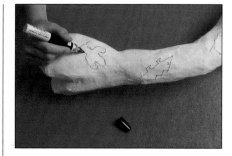

1 When your papier-mâché is completely dry, sketch designs in pencil or with a marker.

2 Choose a background color. Using a medium-sized brush, paint around your designs.

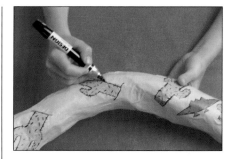

3 Paint inside your designs with the colors of your choice. If you wish to outline your designs, some markers, usually the large-sized waterproof ones, are good for drawing outlines. They can also be painted on with a pointed brush.

Sponge Painting

Sponge painting is an excellent way to soften up a strong color. It is good for creating texture and depth as well. Many colors can be layered over each other for interesting cloud-like patterns.

What You Need
- Paints
- 1 paintbrush
- 1 sponge

1 Choose a background color and paint your project with it.

2 Choose a second color. Using a small square of damp sponge, dip a section of it into the paint and gently squish it onto the background color. Keep squishing it on until you are happy with the results.

Several colors can be layered over each other if you like.

The type of puffy and slick paints that are used for painting on T-shirts are great for adding designs, squiggles and dots to liven up a project. They come in lots of bright and fluorescent colors.

Sponge painting gives this bird texture and makes it more interesting looking.

This bird can be made by following the instructions for the Monsters project. Add a head, beak and wings.

Découpage

Découpage is a great way to get big results with very little effort by cutting designs from wrapping paper, comics, magazines or other printed material and pasting them in place with wallpaper paste.

What You Need
- Paints
- 1 paintbrush
- Wrapping paper, comics or other printed material
- Scissors
- Warm water
- 1 plastic container
- Dry wallpaper paste (a small quantity)

1 When your papier-mâché is completely dry, paint it a solid color. Découpage is easier if the background color of the paint matches the background color of the paper cutouts.

2 Using scissors, cut out images from your wrapping paper.

3 Pour a small amount of warm water into a plastic container. Slowly add pinches of wallpaper paste and mix it with your fingers to eliminate lumps. When the mixture has a soupy consistency, stop mixing. It will get thicker by itself.

4 Smooth some paste on an area of your project. Lay a cutout on the paste. Smooth some more paste over it. Do this gently and don't rub, as it will damage your cutout. Continue until you have enough cutouts in place. Any excess paste will dry clear.

Some patterns and designs look best spread apart.

Designs like the comics on this pig can be used to create a theme. They can be overlapped to completely cover a project, or spaces can be left so that the comics can be read.

The cat above was covered in wrapping paper that has a small, intricate pattern. Try tearing the paper into pieces instead of cutting out designs one at a time. When you apply the torn pieces, overlap them. The overall effect looks as if you covered your project with one big sheet of paper.

Potato Printing

Create a chunky design and repeat it on your project with potato printing. This is a fast, fun, easy way to decorate an object. The patterns created with potato printing are a good size for papier-mâché objects and look like stencilled designs.

What You Need
- Paints
- 1 medium-sized paintbrush
- Small, sharp kitchen knife
- 1 medium to large potato
- Pencil

1 When your papier-mâché is dry, paint it all over with white or a background color.

2 Using a small, sharp kitchen knife, cut the potato in half across its width.
Using the pencil, draw a shape on the cut surface of the potato. Keep it as simple as possible.

3 Using the knife, cut into the potato around your design. Then cut into the sides of the potato and remove the excess potato around the design. The design should now stand up from the rest of the potato.

4 Using your paintbrush, paint the design area of the potato with the color you wish, or dip the potato design into the paint.

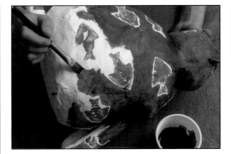

5 Press the surface of the potato design onto the object. You may need to rock it to get an even coverage. Remove the potato and take a look. If the paint is too uneven, you can touch it up a bit with your brush; but remember, it's supposed to be uneven and have some blank spaces in it.

Repeat as many times as you wish.

6 If you like, you can add a different background color around the prints. Dots, squiggles or other designs can also be added.

Pulp

Pulp is a mushy material made from torn toilet paper mixed with paste. It can be used as a kind of clay to make eyes, noses, lips and other features. It can also be used for texture, because it has a pitted surface like concrete when it is dry.

To smooth the texture of the pulp somewhat, see the cornstarch and glue recipe below.

What You Need
- Toilet paper
- 1 mixing bowl
- Flour, salt and water paste (recipe, page 10)

Optional
- Cornstarch
- Small plastic container
- Water
- Carpenter's glue
- Brush or stick

1 Tear 12 sheets of toilet paper one at a time from the roll.
Lay the sheets of toilet paper on top of each other in a stack.

2 Tear the stack of toilet paper into narrow strips.

3 Rip the strips into small pieces.
Hold a bunch of torn pieces loosely in each hand and rub the bunches together to separate the small pieces. If some pieces are still stuck together, separate them as much as possible by hand.

4 Place the toilet paper pieces in a bowl and add a small quantity of flour, salt and water paste.

5 Mush the paste into the toilet paper bits until they are all moist. Don't make the pulp too wet. When you squeeze it between your fingers, no paste should run out.

6 Form the pulp into the shape you want and attach it to your project. It will stick by itself.

7 When the pulp is dry, you may wish to smooth the texture of it somewhat. Do this by coating it with the following mixture:
Place 2 large spoonfuls of cornstarch in a small plastic container.

8 Add 3 large spoonfuls of water. Squeeze some carpenter's glue into the cornstarch and water. Mix with a brush or stick.
The mixture should be thick and gluey. Add more cornstarch to thicken or equal amounts of glue and water to thin.

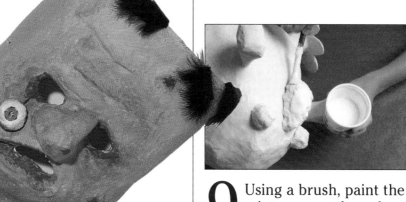

The lumps, bumps and ugly features of this scary mask were made from pulp.

9 Using a brush, paint the mixture over the pulp. Check on it occasionally while it dries to keep it from running.

Baker's Clay

Here is an easy-to-make material that has many uses for lots of different crafts. You probably have the ingredients in your kitchen; however, it can take quite a while to bake, so get permission before you begin. Baker's clay is great for making eyes, horns, tongues, teeth and more.

What You Need
- 2 mixing bowls
- 1½ cups (350 mL) all-purpose flour
- ½ cup (100 mL) cornstarch
- ¼ cup (50 mL) salt
- ¾ cup (200 mL) hot water
- Cookie sheet
- Carpenter's glue

1 In a mixing bowl, mix together the flour and cornstarch.
  In a separate bowl, mix the salt and hot water.
  Add the salt water to the dry ingredients. Mix them with a spoon. The particles should stick together.

2 Lift the dough out and form it into a ball. Knead the ball by squashing it in your hands for 5 to 10 minutes.

3 When the dough is smooth and satiny, form the shapes that you wish. Lay the pieces on an ungreased cookie sheet.
  Bake them in a 200° F (100° C) oven. Small and thin items take about 2 hours to bake, while larger pieces can take 4 hours. Setting a timer or alarm clock to tell you that the time is up is a good idea. If the baker's clay is overcooked, it can become brittle and break very easily.

4 Paint the baker's clay items the colors you wish.

5 Attach them to your project with carpenter's glue.

The snake's eyes and tongue, the pig's tail and the monster's eyes and teeth were all made from baker's clay.

Add-ons

Add-ons are extra bits and pieces and decorations that can be added to your project to make it more interesting or funny. The following are some ideas for add-ons; however, you don't need to stick to what is shown here. Look around the house to find sewing odds and ends, buttons, wool, popsicle sticks or other items that you can use. Stick your add-ons in place with carpenter's glue.

Adding inexpensive pom poms to the spider on the left, and sequins held on by ball-tipped pins to the spider on the right, made them look more humorous and more three dimensional.

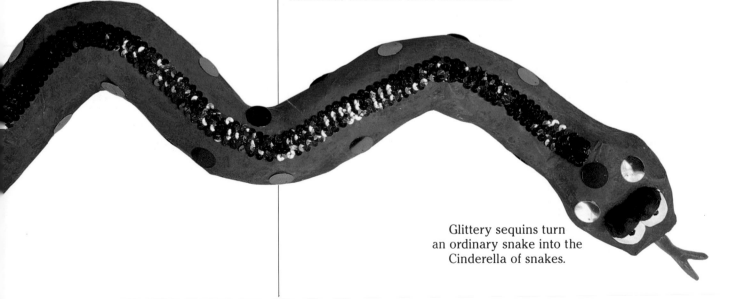

Glittery sequins turn an ordinary snake into the Cinderella of snakes.

It only takes a little fun fur to give a monster some personality. It also makes an icky spider into a cuddly spider.

Feathers can add drama to a mask, or they can be used in place of hair. Feathers can also be glued to the wings of a flying pig or other creature to add realism.

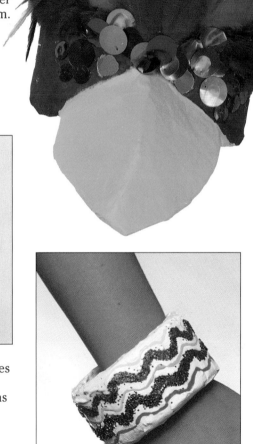

A fake nose from a joke store makes a mask more lifelike. Sunglasses, fake mustaches and other gag items can be used.

Pieces of nylon rope were glued into holes to give this monster its crazy hairdo. Once it was in place, the rope was unraveled.

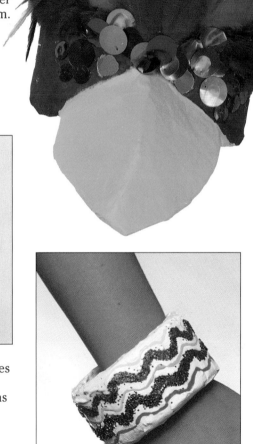

Glitter can add sparkle to a project. Paint carpenter's glue where you want the glitter to stick and pour glitter onto those areas, then shake off the excess. Let it dry.

Sheila McGraw is the author of *Papier-Mâché Today* (Firefly, 1990), the award-winning book of advanced papier-mâché projects. She is also co-author and illustrator of *My Mother's Hands* (Medlicott Press, Simon and Schuster, 1991), author and illustrator of *This Old New House* (Annick Press, 1989) and illustrator of the best-selling children's book *Love You Forever* (Firefly, 1986).